Log Cabin Quilts

By Penny Haren

Log Cabin Quilts
By Penny Haren

Landauer Publishing is an imprint of Fox Chapel Publishing Company, Inc.

President/Publisher: Jeramy Lanigan Landauer
Editors: Jeri Simon; Doris Brunnette
Art Director: Laurel Albright
Photographer: Sue Voegtlin

Library of Congress: 2016938113
ISBN: 978-1-935726-85-2

We are always looking for talented authors. To submit an idea,
please send a brief inquiry to acquisitions@foxchapelpublishing.com

Printed in the United States of America

10-9-8-7-6-5-4-3

Contents

About the Author

For more than 30 years as a quilter, and several years as a quilt shop owner, Ohio-based Penny Haren has been developing and teaching techniques to make creating blocks and projects quick, easy and fun for quilters of all skill levels. She has authored several books teaching her original Pieced Appliqué® technique.

Penny also designs rulers for Creative Grids® and has developed a line of quality notions available through independent quilt shops. In addition, she consults and writes the newsletter for Checker Distributors®.

Penny is the mother of four sons, one daughter and three "bonus" daughters. She is also the proud grandmother of six and foster grandmother of two.

If you would like Penny to teach at your shop or guild, contact her at pennyharen70@hotmail.com.

A special thanks to Cheryl Lorence for machine quilting the projects in this book.

Introduction

Log cabin quilts are the original scrap quilts and arguably the most popular design of all time. They are a true study in darks and lights. All fabrics work well in the blocks and ultimately the pattern. Country fabrics create a traditional look while contemporary fabrics give log cabin quilts a modern vibe.

A few discoveries I made while sewing

- Approximately 24" of light fabric and 30" of dark fabric are required for each block. This is actually more than you need, but it's a good starting point.
- A twin-size quilt (72" x 90") used almost 9 yards of fabric from my stash.
- Chain piecing and the Creative Grids® 6" Log Cabin Trim Tool allowed me to make multiple log cabin blocks in a short amount of time.
- An 'organized' stash is a big time-saver.

Organizing A Fabric Stash

For the longest time my entire fabric stash was organized by color— a drawer for red, a drawer for blue, a drawer for green…you get the picture. Since the quilts I wanted to create out of my stash were scrap quilts, this organizational system was not working for me.

Before reorganizing, I took a few minutes to look at my entire stash. This helped determine how I should sort my fabrics. My stash is now sorted by fabric types—a bin for country, a bin for batiks, a bin for neutrals…once again, you get the picture. While sorting my stash, any large scraps were cut into 5" and 10" strips and set aside for layer cake and charm projects. Anything less than 5" was cut into 1-1/2" strips for log cabin blocks.

Once I reorganized my stash, these scrappy log cabin quilts went together beautifully.

Adding Wool to the Projects

I also have many scraps of wool that I have collected over the years. I love them all and wanted to use them in the log cabin projects. The quilts are beautiful before adding the wool, so you may choose not to use it.

Before adding wool to the quilts, ensure that it is colorfast. To test for colorfastness, place a scrap of wool and a piece of white cotton fabric in warm water. The wool will bleed onto the white cotton fabric if it is not colorfast. If the wool is not colorfast, drop wool pieces of the same color into a pan of boiling water for a few minutes and then immerse them in cold water. Throw the pieces in the dryer on a high heat setting.

To cut multiple numbers of the same wool shape, staple the freezer paper template to several layers of wool at one time. Use a very sharp scissors to cut out the shapes. I also like to use a water-soluble glue stick to hold the wool shapes in place while I appliqué them to the quilt top. This also saves time.

I'm sure you are going to discover that creating log cabin quilts is addictive. I know I did.

Penny

Blocks from Scraps and Strips Using the 6" Log Cabin Trim Tool

I piece my blocks two different ways. For small projects I cut the logs according to the chart below; these measurements are the minimum size needed to use with the 6" Log Cabin Trim Tool. If you prefer to use fat quarters for your blocks, see Using Fat Quarters below. I organize the fabric placement before I start piecing to ensure even distribution of colors and values throughout the block. When using scraps from my stash for a larger project, I prefer to chain piece from strips (Pages 18-27).

 6" Finished Log Cabin Block		 6" Finished Courthouse Steps Block		 6" Finished Square-in-a-Square Block		 6" Finished Half-Log Cabin Block	
Center	2" Square	Center	2" Square	Center	2" Light Square	Corner	2" Square
Round 1		**Round 1**		**Round 1**		**Round 1**	
Light	(1) 1-½" x 2"	Light	(2) 1-½" x 2"	Dark	(2) 1-½" x 2"	Light	(1) 1-½" x 2"
	(1) 1-½" x 3"	Dark	(2) 1-½" x 4"	Dark	(2) 1-½" x 4"	Dark	(1) 1-½" x 3"
Dark	(1) 1-½" x 3"						
	(1) 1-½" x 4"	**Round 2**		**Round 2**		**Round 2**	
		Light	(2) 1-½" x 3-½"	Light	(2) 1-½" x 3-½"	Light	(1) 1-½" x 2-¾"
Round 2		Dark	(2) 1-½" x 5-½"	Light	(2) 1-½" x 5-½"	Dark	(1) 1-½" x 3-¾"
Light	(1) 1-½" x 3-½"						
	(1) 1-½" x 4-½"	**Round 3**		**Round 3**		**Round 3**	
Dark	(1) 1-½" x 4-½"	Light	(2) 1-½" x 5"	Dark	(2) 1-½" x 5"	Light	(1) 1-½" x 3-½"
	(1) 1-½" x 5-½"	Dark	(2) 1-½" x 7"	Dark	(2) 1-½" x 7"	Dark	(1) 1-½" x 4-½"
Round 3							
Light	(1) 1-½" x 5"					**Round 4**	
	(1) 1-½" x 6"					Light	(1) 1-½" x 4-¼"
Dark	(1) 1-½" x 6"					Dark	(1) 1-½" x 5-¼"
	(1) 1-½" x 7"						
						Round 5	
						Light	(1) 1-½" x 5"
						Dark	(1) 1-½" x 6"
						Round 6	
						Light	(1) 1-½" x 5-¾"
						Dark	(1) 1-½" x 6-¾"

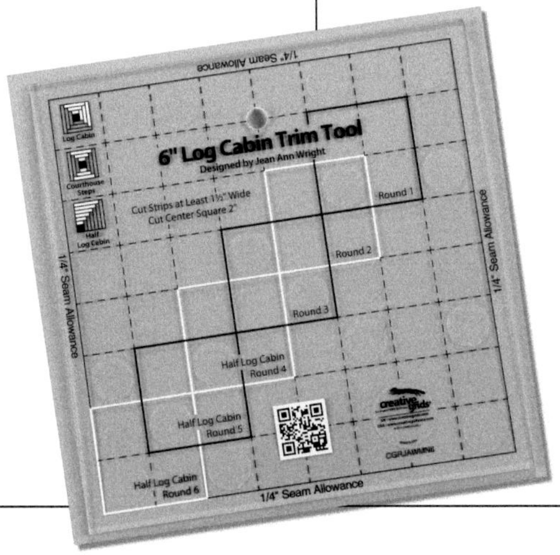

Using Fat Quarters

Centers

A fat quarter measures approximately 18" x 21" and will yield (9) 2" x 21" strips. Each strip can be cut into (10) 2" squares. One fat quarter will yield (90) 2" centers.

Logs

A fat quarter will yield (12) 1-½" x 21" strips. When chain piecing this is enough to make light logs for 10 log cabin blocks and dark logs for 8 log cabin blocks.

To achieve a scrappy look you will need an assortment of 6 light and 6 dark fat quarters. This will be enough fabric to make approximately 48 log cabin blocks.

Making Blocks with the 6" Log Cabin Trim Tool

The 6" Log Cabin Trim Tool allows you to make perfect Log Cabin, Half Log Cabin and Courthouse Steps blocks quickly and easily, guaranteeing success for a beginner! Logs can be cut to size according to the chart on Page 5, however that is not necessary. After each round is sewn the logs are trimmed to size using the 6" Log Cabin Trim Tool. One side of the fabric log needs to be rotary cut and the logs need to be at least 1-1/2"-wide; at this width, there is minimal fabric waste when trimming. If I have wider scrap strips, as shown in step 1 below, I use them. I would rather turn my stash into a beautiful quilt than wait for the perfect project that requires the wider strips! For a quick way to make multiple log cabin blocks, refer to Chain Piecing Log Cabin Blocks on pages 18-21.

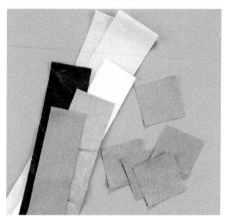

1 Cut 2" squares for the center of each log cabin block. Rotary cut at least one side of the logs so you have a straight edge. The logs need to be cut at least 1-½"-wide. Cut an assortment of light and dark value strips for logs.

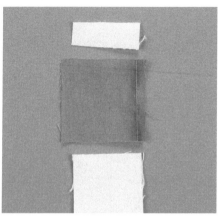

2 With right sides together, align a center square with the rotary cut edge of a light value log. Stitch along the edge using a ¼" seam allowance. Trim the log even with the center square. Press seam toward the log.

3 With right sides together, align the rotary cut edge of a light value log on the adjacent side of the center square, overlapping the previously added log. Stitch along the edge using a ¼" seam allowance.

4 Trim the log even with the center square. Press seam toward the log.

Note: From this point forward, place the center square on top of the log you are adding to help control the direction of your seams for smoother pressing as you sew.

5 Sew the dark value logs on the remaining two adjacent sides of the center square to finish sewing Round 1. Press seams toward logs.

Note: The ends of each new log should overlap the edges of the previous round just a bit. This allows you to trim each new round.

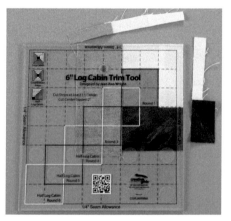

6 Position the Round 1 square of the trim tool on the center square. Trim the two light sides along the right and upper edges.

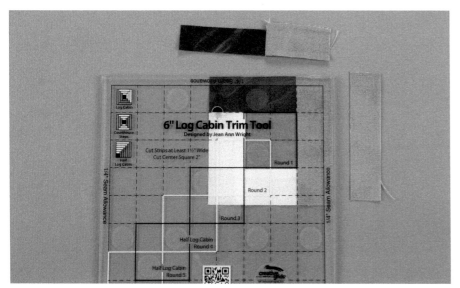

8 Round 1 is complete and you are ready to add Round 2.

7 Turn the block 180-degrees and reposition the Round 1 square of the trim tool on the center square. Trim the two dark sides along the right and upper edges.

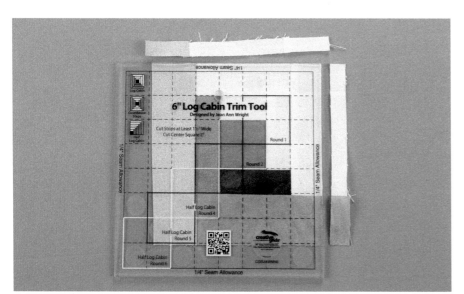

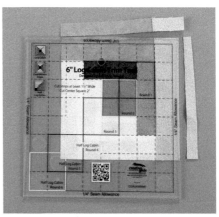

10 Turn the block 180-degrees and reposition the Round 2 square on the center square as shown. Trim the two dark sides along the right and upper edges of the trim tool.

9 Sew two light value logs and two dark value logs to complete Round 2. Press seams toward the log.

Position the Round 2 square on the center square and trim the two light sides along the right and upper edges of the trim tool.

11 Round 2 is complete and you are ready to add Round 3.

12 Sew two light value logs and two dark value logs to complete Round 3. Press seam toward the log as you sew each seam.

Position the Round 3 square on the center square and trim the two light sides along the right and upper edges of the trim tool.

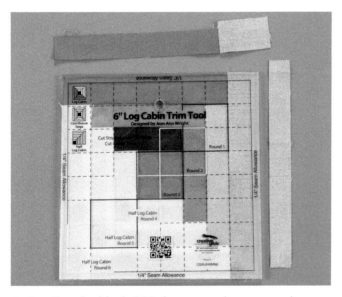

Finished Log Cabin Block

13 Turn the block 180-degrees and reposition the Round 3 square of the trim tool on the center square. Trim the two dark sides along the right and upper edges of the trim tool.

Courthouse Steps Block

1 Cut precise 2" squares for the center of each Courthouse Steps Block. Rotary cut at least one side of the logs so you have a straight edge. The logs need to be cut at least 1-1/2"-wide. Cut an assortment of light and dark value strips for logs.

2 With right sides together, align a center square with the rotary cut edge of a light value log. Stitch along the edge using a 1/4" seam allowance. Repeat with a light value log on the opposite side of the center square. Trim light value logs even with the center square. Press seams toward the log.

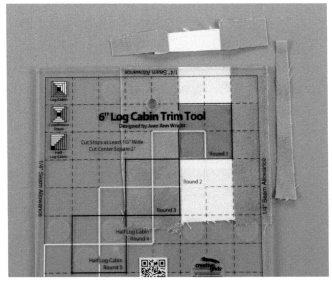

3 Place the pieced unit on top of a dark value log, right sides together. Stitch along the edge using a 1/4" seam allowance. Repeat with a dark value log on the opposite side of the center square. Press seam toward the log.

4 Position the Round 1 square on the center square. Trim along the right and upper edges of the trim tool.

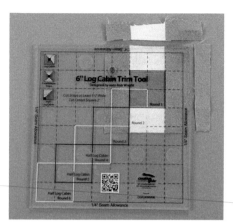

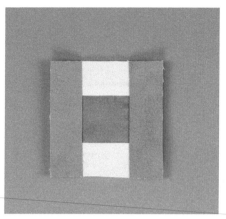

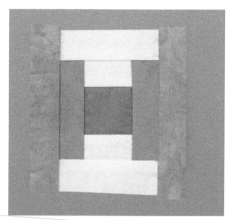

5 Turn the block 180-degrees and reposition the Round 1 square on the center square. Trim along the right and upper edges of the trim tool.

6 Round 1 is complete and you are ready to add Round 2.

7 Sew two light value logs and two dark value logs to complete Round 2. Press seams toward the logs.

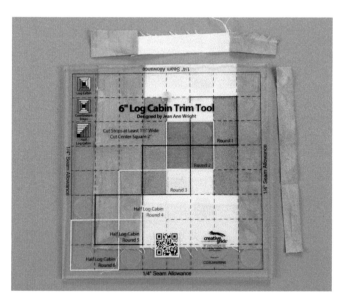

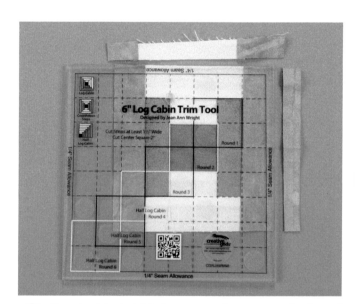

8 Position the Round 2 square on the center square and trim along the right and upper edges of the trim tool.

9 Turn the block 180-degrees and reposition the Round 2 square on the center square. Trim along the right and upper edges of the trim tool.

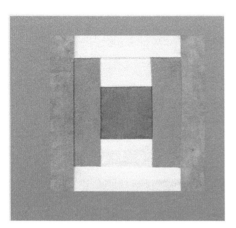

10 Round 2 is complete and you are ready to add Round 3.

11 Sew two light value logs and two dark value logs to complete Round 2. Press seams toward the logs.

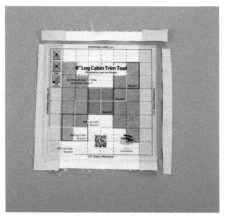

12 Position the Round 3 square on the center square. Trim along the right and upper edges of the trim tool.

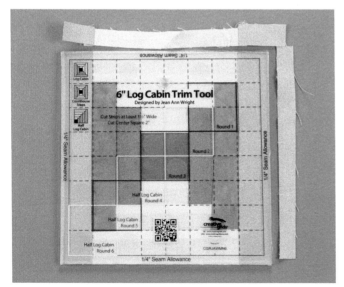

13 Turn the block 180-degrees and reposition the Round 3 square on the center square. Trim along the right and upper edges of the trim tool.

Finished Courthouse Steps Block

1 Cut precise 2" squares for the corner of each Half Log Cabin Block. Rotary cut one side of the fabric strips so you have a straight edge. The strips need to be cut at least 1-1/2"-wide for the logs. Cut an assortment of light and dark value strips for logs.

2 With right sides together, align a corner square with the rotary cut edge of a light value log. Stitch along the edge using a 1/4" seam allowance. Trim light value log even with the center square. Press seam toward the log.

3 With right sides together, align the rotary cut edge of a dark value log on the adjacent side of the corner square. Stitch along the edge using a 1/4" seam allowance. Press seam toward the log.

Note: From this point forward, place the corner square on top of the log you are adding to help control the direction of your seams for smoother pressing as you sew.

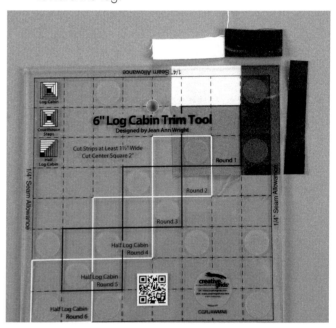

4 Position the Round 1 square on the corner square as shown. Trim along the right and upper edges of the trim tool. The other two sides of the block will be trimmed after all logs have been added.

5 Round 1 is complete and you are ready to add Round 2.

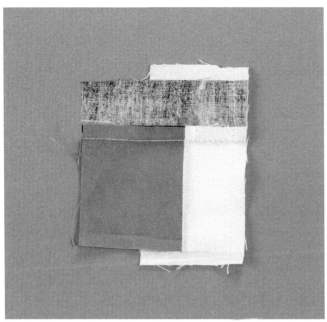

6 Sew u light value log to the block, aligning it with the light value log from Round 1. Trim light value log even with the Round 1 dark value log. Sew a dark value log on the adjacent side of the block aligning it with the dark value log from Round 1. Press seams toward the logs.

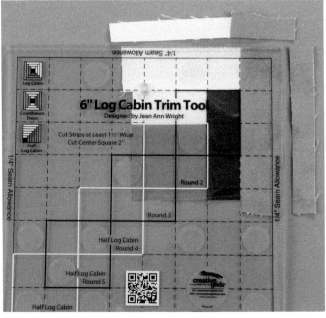

7 Position the Round 2 square on the corner square as shown. Trim along the right and upper edges of the trim tool.

8 Round 2 is complete and you are ready to add Round 3.

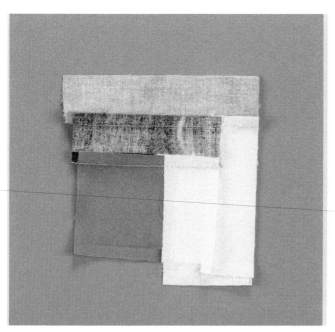

9 Sew a light value log to the block, aligning it with the light value log from Round 2. Trim light value log even with the Round 2 dark value log. Sew a dark value log on the adjacent side of the block aligning it with the dark value log from Round 2. Press seams toward the logs.

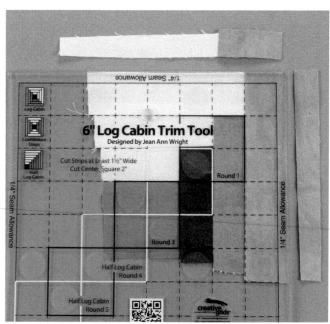

10 Position the Round 3 square on the corner square as shown. Trim along the right and upper edges of the trim tool.

11 Round 3 is complete and you are ready to add Round 4.

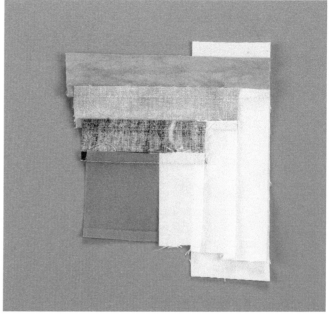

12 Sew a light value log to the block, aligning it with the light value log from Round 3. Trim light value log even with the Round 3 dark value log. Sew a dark value log on the adjacent side of the block aligning it with the dark value log from Round 3. Press seams toward the logs.

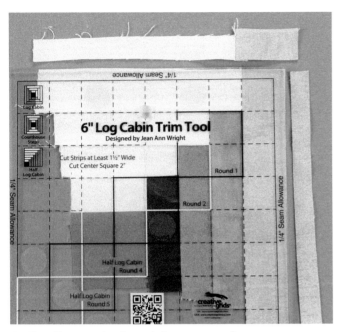

13 Position the Round 4 square on the corner square as shown. Trim along the right and upper edges of the trim tool.

14 Round 4 is complete and you are ready to add Round 5.

15 Sew a light value log to the block, aligning it with the light value log from Round 4. Sew a dark value log on the adjacent side of the block aligning it with the dark value log from Round 4. Press seams toward the logs.

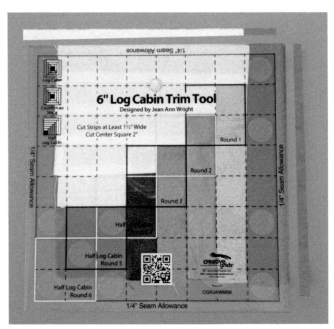

16 Position the Round 5 square on the corner square. Trim along the right and upper edges of the trim tool.

17 Round 5 is complete and you are ready to add Round 6.

18 Sew a light value log to the block, aligning it with the light value log from Round 5. Sew a dark value log on the adjacent side of the block aligning it with the dark value log from Round 5. Press seams toward the logs.

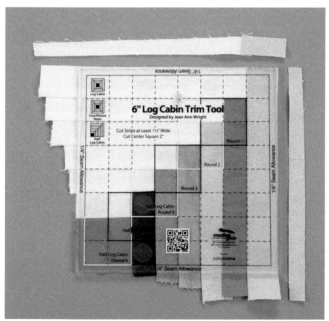

19 Position the Round 6 square on the corner square as shown. Trim along the right and upper edges of the trim tool.

20 Round 6 is complete and ready to trim the other two sides.

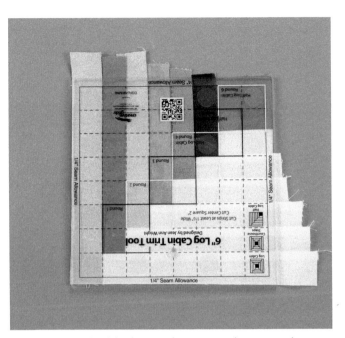

21 Turn the block 180-degrees and position the Round 6 square on the corner square as shown.

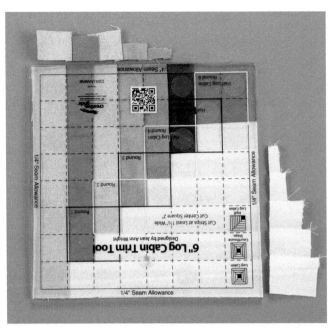

22 Trim along the right and upper edges of the trim tool.

23 The Half Log Cabin Block should measure 6-1/2".

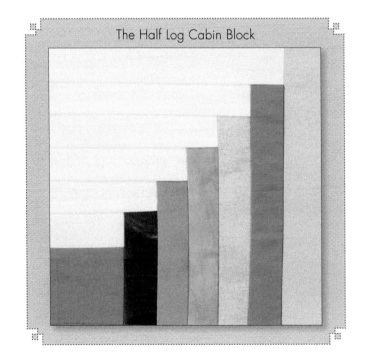

The Half Log Cabin Block

Chain Piecing Log Cabin Blocks

The techniques on the previous pages do not change with chain piecing; logs have to be at least 1-1/2"-wide and seams are always pressed toward the log. But sewing multiple segments at one time is a quick and easy way to make multiple numbers of Log Cabin blocks in a snap. And strip sets can be stacked to cut multiple segments, making the process even faster!

1 Cut a 2" x wof dark strip and an assortment of 1-1/2" x wof light and dark strips. The 2" strip is for the center squares. The 1-1/2" strips are for the logs.

wof = width of fabric

2 Sew a 1-1/2" light strip to one side of a 2" dark strip along one long edge. Press seam toward the light strip to make a strip set. The light strip is the first log.

3 Cut the strip set into 2" segments.

Note: Multiple strip sets can be stacked to cut the segments.

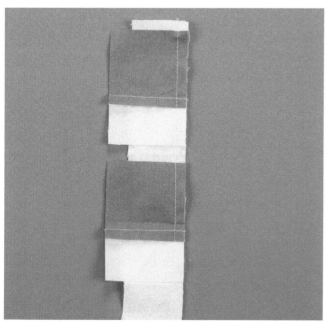

4 Place a segment on top of a light strip, right sides together. As you sew, continue to add segments to the light strip, leaving space between for cutting.

5 Cut the segments apart, trimming even with light strip.

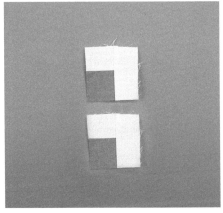

6 Press seam toward the light strip.

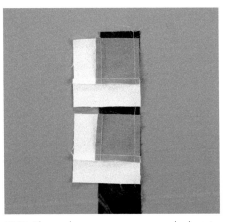

7 Place the segments on a dark strip, right sides together. As you sew, leave space between for cutting.

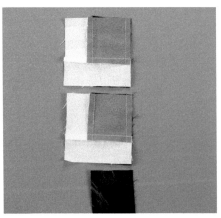

8 Cut the segments apart, trimming even with the pieced unit.

9 Press seam toward the dark strip.

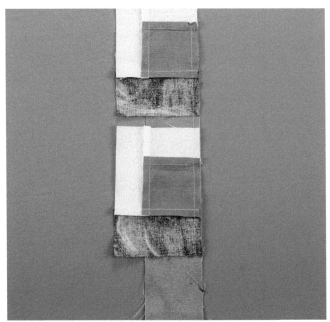

10 Place the segments on a dark strip, right sides together. As you sew, leave space between for cutting.

11 Cut the segments apart, trimming even with the dark strip. Press seam toward the dark strip to complete Round 1.

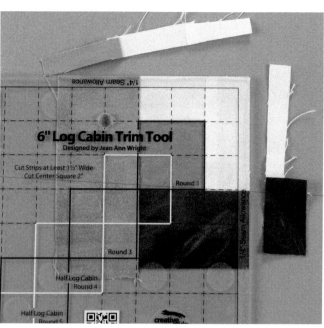

12 Position the Round 1 square on the center square. Trim along the right and upper edges of the trim tool.

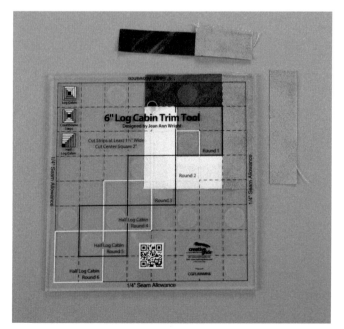

13 Turn the block 180-degrees and reposition the Round 1 square on the center square. Trim along the right and upper edges of the trim tool.

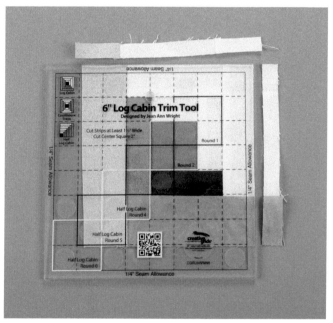

14 In the same manner, sew an additional 2 light and 2 dark strips to the block to complete Round 2. Position the Round 2 square on the center square and trim the two light sides along the right and upper edges of the trim tool.

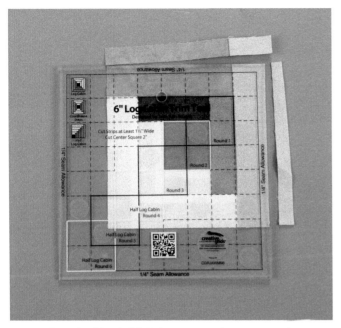

15 Turn the block 180-degrees and reposition the Round 2 square on the center square. Trim along the right and upper edges of the trim tool.

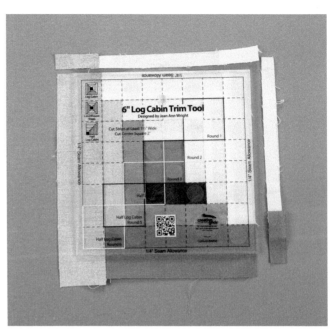

16 Sew an additional 2 light and 2 dark strips to the block to complete Round 3. Position the Round 3 square on the center square and trim the two light sides along the right and upper edges of the trim tool.

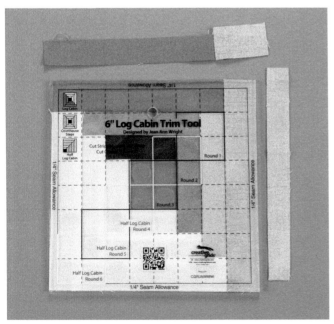

17 Turn the block 180-degrees and reposition the Round 3 square on the center square. Trim along the right and upper edges of the trim tool. The Log Cabin Block should measure 6-1/2".

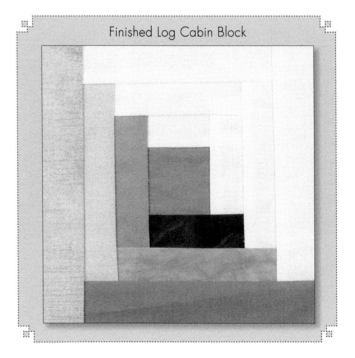

Finished Log Cabin Block

1 Cut a 2" x wof dark strip and an assortment of 1-1/2" x wof light and dark strips. The 2" strip is for the center squares. The 1-1/2" strips are for the logs.

wof = width of fabric

2 Sew a 1-1/2" light strip on either side of the 2" dark strip along the long edges. Press seam toward the light strip to make a strip set. The light strips are the first logs.

3 Cut the strip set into 2" segments.

Note: Multiple strip sets can be stacked to cut the segments.

4 Place a segment on top of a light strip, right sides together. As you sew, continue to add segments to the light strip, leaving space between for cutting.

5 Cut the segments apart, trimming even with the dark strip.

6 Press seam toward the dark strip. Since you are not crossing seams when sewing the next dark strip, you can wait and press after both dark strips have been added.

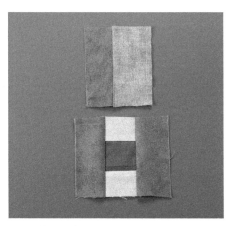

7 Place the segments on top of a dark strip, right sides together. As you sew, leave space between the segments for cutting. Cut the segments apart, trimming even with the light strip. Press seams toward the dark value log.

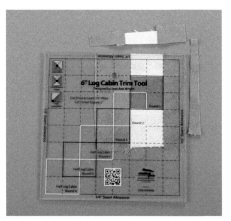

8 Position the Round 1 square on the center square. Trim along the right and upper edges of the trim tool.

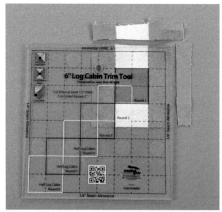

9 Turn the block 180-degrees and reposition the Round 1 square on the center square. Trim along the right and upper edges of the trim tool.

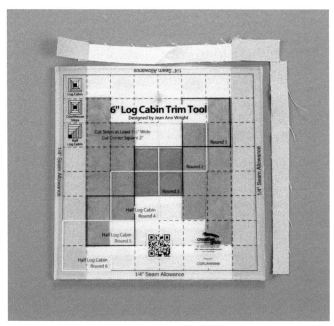

10 Continue adding light and dark strips to opposite sides of the center square. Trim each round with the corresponding square of the 6" Log Cabin Trim Tool. The Courthouse Steps Block should measure 6-1/2".

Finished Courthouse Steps Block

1 Cut a 2" x wof dark strip and an assortment of 1-1/2" x wof light and dark strips. The 2" strip is for the corner squares. The 1-1/2" strips are for the logs. The logs need to be cut at least 1-½-wide. Cut an assortment of light and dark value strips for logs.

wof = width of fabric

2 Sew a 1-1/2" light strip to one side of a 2" dark strip along one edge. Press seam toward the light strip to make a strip set. The light strip is the first log.

3 Cut the strip set into 2" segments.

Note: Multiple strip sets can be stacked to cut the segments.

4 Place a segment on top of a dark strip, right sides together. As you sew, continue to add segments to the dark strip, leaving space between for cutting.

5 Cut the segments apart, trimming even with the pieced unit.

6 Press seam toward the dark strip.

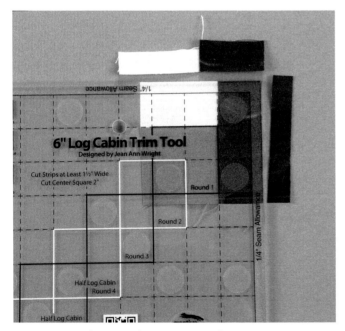

7 Position the Round 1 square on the corner square. Trim along the right and upper edges of the trim tool.

Note: There is no need to trim the bottom and left side of the block until all rounds have been added.

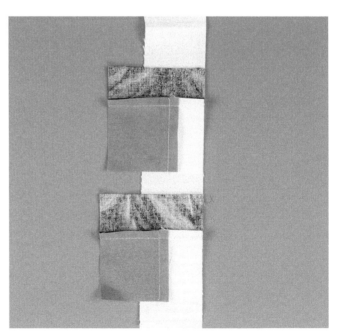

8 Place a segment on top of a light strip, right sides together. As you sew, continue to add segments to the light strip, leaving space between for cutting.

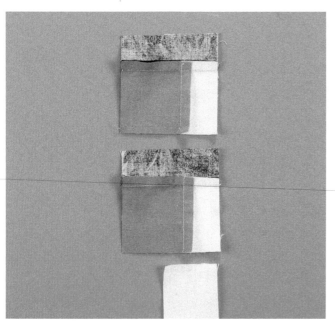

9 Cut the segments apart, trimming even with pieced unit.

10 Press seam toward the light strip.

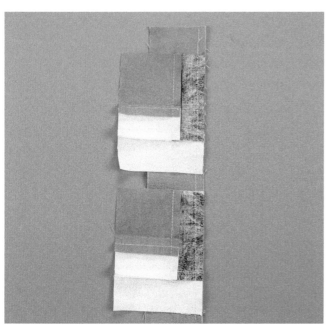

11 Place a segment on top of a dark strip, right sides together. As you sew, continue to add segments to the dark strip, leaving space between for cutting.

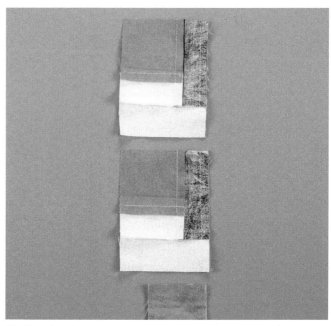

12 Cut the segments apart, trimming even with pieced unit.

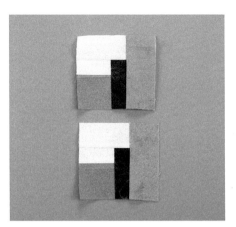

13 Press seam toward the dark strip to complete Round 2.

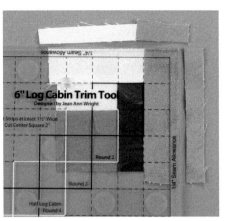

14 Position the Round 2 square on the corner square. Trim along the right and upper edges of the trim tool.

15 Continue adding light and dark strips; light strips should be on one side of the corner square and dark strips on the adjacent side. Trim each round with the corresponding square on the trim tool. The Half Log Cabin Block has six rounds of strips.

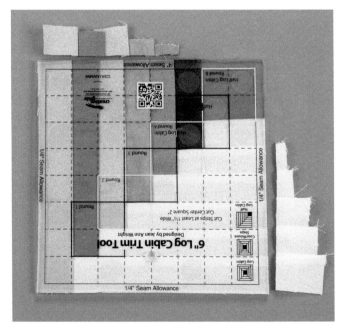

16 Turn the block 180-degrees and reposition the Round 6 square on the center square. Trim along the right and upper edges of the trim tool. The Half Log Cabin Block should measure 6-1/2".

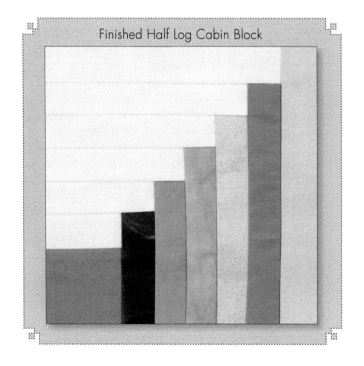

Finished Half Log Cabin Block

Cabin on the Lake Quilt

Finished Quilt Size: 73-1/2" x 97-1/2"

For over 100 years, log cabin quilts have warmed the heart and soul of many. With all its tradition, it remains a favorite, whether in a country setting or a contemporary city high-rise. It speaks of home wherever it is found

Materials

- 1/2 yard black print fabric
- 4 yards assorted light value fabrics
- 4-1/2 yards assorted dark value fabrics
- 2-2/3 yards assorted medium and dark print fabrics
- 1 yard dark red fabric
- 1/2 yard red wool (60"-wide)
- 6 yards backing fabric
- Queen-size batting
- Freezer paper

Read through Making Blocks with the 6" Log Cabin Trim Tool and Chain Piecing Log Cabin Blocks on pages 6-27 before beginning.

wof = width of fabric

Cutting

From black print fabric, cut:
  (140) 2" corner squares

From assorted light value fabrics, cut:
  1-1/2" x wof strips for blocks

From assorted dark value fabrics, cut:
  1-1/2" x wof strips for blocks

From assorted medium and dark print fabrics, cut:
  (40) 2-1/2" x wof strips for pieced outer border

From dark red fabric, cut:
  (8) 1-1/4" x wof inner border strips
  (9) 2-1/4" x wof binding strips

Making the Blocks

Note: Refer to pages 12-17 and 24-27 to sew the Half Log Cabin Blocks.

1. Sew a 2" black center square to a light strip, right sides together. Trim the light strip even with the corner square and press the seam.

2. Sew the segment from step 1 to a 1-1/2" dark strip, right sides together. The strips should be sewn in a clockwise rotation on adjacent sides of the black corner square. Trim the dark strip slightly longer than the corner square to complete Round 1.

3. Press the block and trim Round 1 to size using the 6" Log Cabin Trim Tool.

4. Referring to steps 2-3, sew rounds 2-6 to the block. Press and trim the block after each round is added. Make 140 Half Log Cabin Blocks.

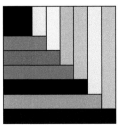

Make 140

Row Assembly

1. Lay out the Half Log Cabin Blocks in 14 rows with 10 blocks in each row. Carefully watch the orientation of the blocks.

2. Sew the blocks together in rows. Press the seams in the odd numbered rows to the left and the seams in the even numbered rows to the right.

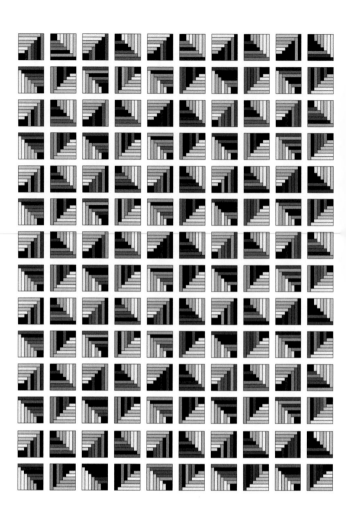

3. Sew rows 2-13 together in pairs, nesting the seams. Make 6 row pairs. Rows 1 and 14 will be added later. Press the seams open to relieve bulk when adding the appliqués.

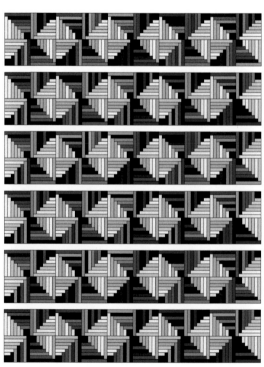

Adding the Appliqué

Note: There are 24 houses on the featured quilt.
The shapes are appliquéd on the row pairs.

1. Trace the appliqué shapes on page 34
    onto the matte side of the freezer paper.
    Cut out the shapes.

2. Press the shiny side of the freezer paper to the
    red wool. Cut out the wool shapes.

Note: The freezer paper will help stabilize the wool
making it easier to cut.

3. Referring to the Appliqué Placement Diagram,
    position the roof shape on the Log Cabin
    Blocks. Place the remaining two house pieces
    approximately 1/4" from the roof. Remove
    the freezer paper and glue the wool pieces in
    place using water-soluble glue.

4. Appliqué the shapes in place using an
    invisible appliqué stitch.

Quilt Center Assembly

1. Referring to the Quilt Center Assembly
    Diagram, lay out the row pairs and rows 1
    and 14 as shown.

2. Sew the rows together to complete the
    quilt center. Press seams open.

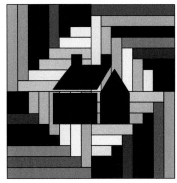

Appliqué Placement Diagram

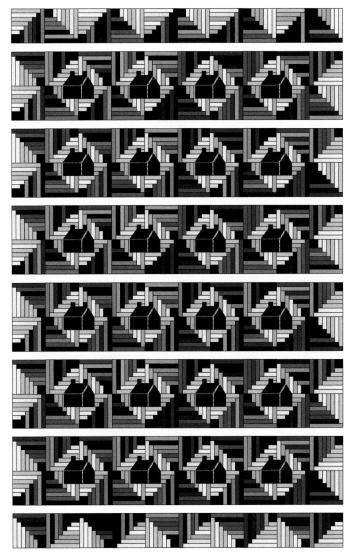

Quilt Center Assembly Diagram

Adding the Borders

Inner Border

1. Sew the 1-1/4" x wof inner border strips together on the diagonal to make one strip.

2. Measure the length of the quilt center and cut two strips to that length. The strips should measure approximately 84-1/2". Sew the strips to opposite sides of the quilt center.

3. Measure the width of the quilt center including side borders and cut two strips to that length. The strips should measure approximately 62". Sew the strips to the top and bottom of the quilt center.

Pieced Outer Border

1. Layer (2) 2-1/2" x wof outer border strips right sides together.

2. Using a 1/4" seam, sew the strips together along each long edge to make a tube. Make 20 tubes.

Make 20

3. Cut each tube into (6) 6-1/2" segments. The tubes can be stacked when cutting the segments. Cut (120) 6-1/2" segments.

4. Cut each 6-1/2" segment in half lengthwise. Each segment should measure approximately 6-1/2" x 1-1/4" before pressing open.

5. Press the seams open for a total of 240 strip units. Set aside 4 strip units. You will have extra strip units.

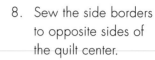

Make 240

6. Sew the remaining strip units together in sets of 4 to make rail fence units. Each rail fence unit should have 8 strips and measure 6-1/2" square. Make 56 rail fence units.

Make 56

7. Sew 14 rail fence units together to make a side border. Press seams open. Sew a strip unit set aside in step 5 to one end of the side border. Make 2 side borders.

8. Sew the side borders to opposite sides of the quilt center.

9. Sew 10 rail fence units together to make a top/bottom border. Press seams open. Sew a strip unit set aside in step 5 to one end of the top/bottom border. Make 2 top/bottom borders.

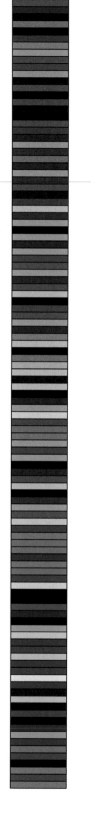

10. Draw a diagonal line on the wrong side of a remaining rail fence unit. Place the unit on another rail fence unit, right sides together.

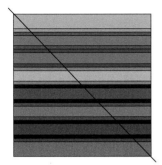

11. Fold the marked unit back to form a right angle. Match the seams in the strip sets and lightly press. Using a water-soluble glue stick to keep the seams in place, lightly glue the unit in place.

12. Unfold the unit and stitch on the drawn line. Trim 1/4" from the stitched line.

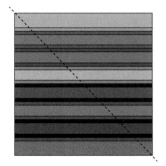 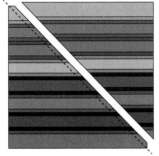

13. Press the seam open. Repeat with the remaining rail fence units to make 4 border corners.

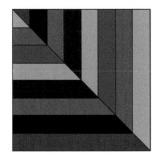

14. Sew a border corner to opposite ends of the top/bottom borders.

15. Sew the top/bottom borders to the top and bottom of the quilt center to complete the quilt top.

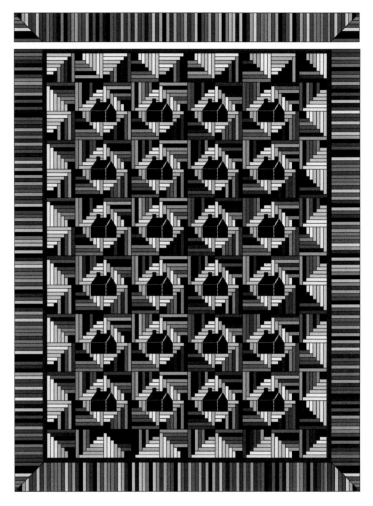

Finishing

1. Layer the quilt top, batting and backing. Quilt as desired.

2. Sew the binding strips together along the short ends to make one strip. Press seams open.

3. Press the strip in half lengthwise, wrong sides together, and sew to the raw edge of the quilt top. Fold binding strip over raw edge and hand stitch in place.

Templates are full-size
Trace 24 of each shape

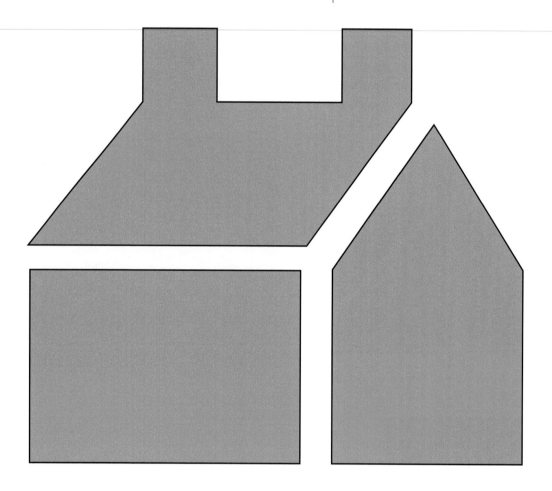

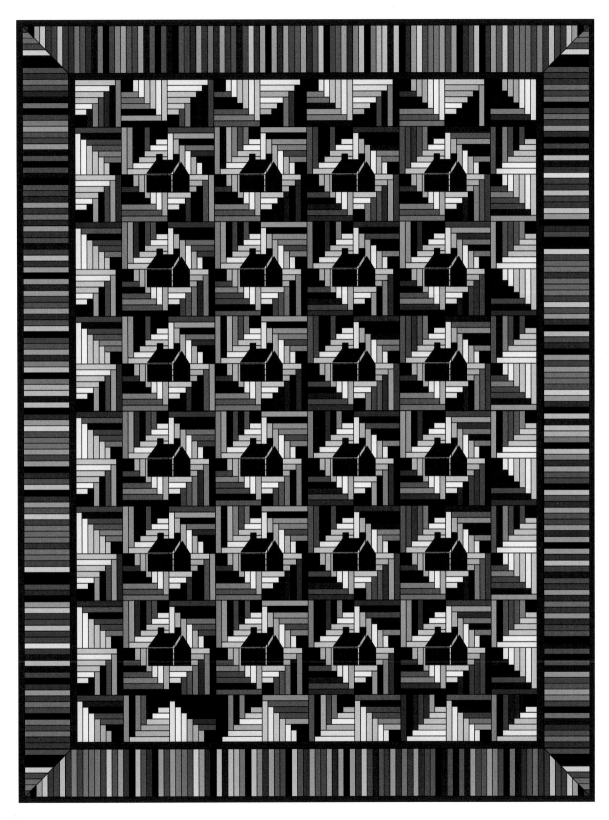

Cabin on the Lake Quilt

Finished Quilt Size: 73-1/2" x 97-1/2"

Welcome Home Mini Quilt

Finished Size: 20" x 24"

With all the hustle and bustle of our daily lives, home has become a sanctuary. This little framed quilt is a reminder of home and what it means to us.

Materials

- (6) assorted light 1-1/2" x wof strips
- (6) assorted dark 1-1/2" x wof strips

Note: For a scrappier look, use a greater variety of light and dark strips.

- (4) dark red 2" center squares
- 1/4 yard cream fabric
- 1/2 yard black fabric
- 4" and 6" squares red wool
- Green #8 perle cotton
- Assorted buttons
- Black Pigma® Micron Pen #08
- 20" x 24" stretched canvas
- Freezer paper

Refer to Making Blocks with the 6" Log Cabin Trim Tool and Chain Piecing Log Cabin Blocks on pages 6-27 before beginning.

wof = width of fabric

Cutting

From cream fabric, cut:
    (2) 2" x 12-1/2" side inner border strips
    (1) 2" x 15-1/2" top inner border strip
    (1) 6" x 15-1/2" bottom inner border strip

From black fabric, cut:
    (2) 5-1/4" x 19-1/2" side outer border strips
    (2) 5-1/4" x 25" top/bottom outer border strips
    (4) circles for yo-yos using the template
       on page 39

Making the Blocks

Note: Since there are only four blocks in this project, I prefer to precut the logs using the chart on page 5 so I can control the placement of the fabrics. Refer to pages 6-8 and 18-21 to sew the blocks.

1. Sew a 2" dark center square to a 1-1/2" light strip, right sides together. Trim the light strip even with the center square and press the seam.

2. Sew the segment from step 1 to another 1-1/2" light strip, right sides together. The light strips should be sewn in a clockwise rotation on adjacent sides of the dark center square. Trim the light strip even with the center square and press the seam.

3. In the same manner, sew two dark strips to the remaining sides of the center square to complete Round 1. Press the block and trim Round 1 to size using the 6" Log Cabin Trim Tool.

4. Referring to steps 2-3, sew Rounds 2 and 3 to the block. Press and trim the block after each round is added. Make 4 light/dark log cabin blocks.

Center Block Assembly

1. Lay out 4 log cabin blocks in 2 rows with 2 blocks in each row. Sew the blocks together in rows, pressing seams in one row to the left and seams in the other row to the right.

2. Sew the rows together, nesting the seams, to complete the center block.

Adding the Borders

Inner Border

1. Sew the 2" x 12-1/2" side inner border strips to opposite sides of the center block. Press seams toward the inner border.

2. Sew the 2" x 15-1/2" top inner border strip to the top of the center block. Sew the 6" x 15-1/2" bottom inner border strip to the bottom of the center block. Press seams toward inner border to complete the quilt center.

Outer Border

1. Sew the 5-1/4" x 19-1/2" side outer border strips to opposite sides of the quilt center. Press seams toward the inner border.

2. Sew the 5-1/4" x 25" top/bottom outer border strips to the top and bottom of the quilt center. Press seams toward the inner border to complete the quilt top.

Adding Words

1. Trace the words on page 38 onto copy paper. Tape the copy paper to a light box or window and place the quilt top over it to ensure the lettering is in the correct position. Refer to the photo on page 36 and the diagram on page 38 for placement. You may wish to use glue to hold the paper in place on the quilt center while tracing.

2. Using the black Pigma® pen, trace the words onto the quilt center. Press with an iron to seal the ink. Remove the paper.

Adding the Appliqué

1. Trace the appliqué shapes on page 39 onto the matte side of the freezer paper. Cut out the shapes.

2. Press the shiny side of the freezer paper to the red wool squares. Cut out the wool shapes.

Note: The freezer paper will help stabilize the wool making it easier to cut.

3. Referring to the diagram on page 38, position the shapes on the quilt center. Remove the freezer paper and glue the shapes in place using water-soluble glue.

4. Appliqué the shapes in place using an invisible appliqué stitch.

Making the Yo-Yos

1. Finger press the edges of the yo-yo circles a scant 1/8" to the wrong side of the fabric. Make running stitches close to the fold using one strand of thread.

2. Pull the strand of thread tight to create a gathered circle on the right side of the fabric. The back of the yo-yo should be flat. Knot the thread and bury it in the fold of the yo-yo. Make 4 yo-yos.

Finishing

1. Using a water-soluble marker, draw the vine around the center block. Embroider the vine with a stem stitch, adding some lazy daisy stitches for the leaves.

2. Attach the yo-yos to the corners of the center block. Sew a button in the center of each yo-yo. Add additional buttons along the vine.

3. Center and stretch the quilt top over the canvas. Staple in place.

Welcome Home Mini Quilt
Finished Size: 20" x 24"

your story begins at home...

Templates are full-size

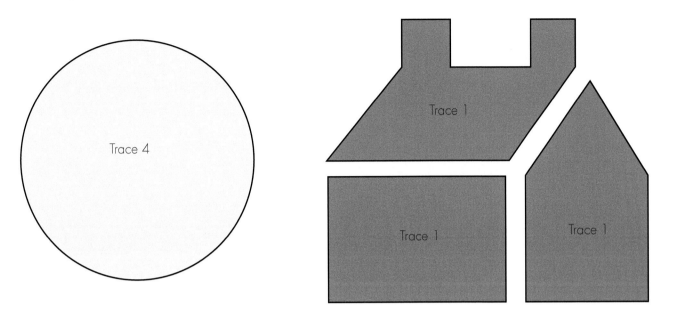

Trace 4

Trace 1

Trace 1

Trace 1

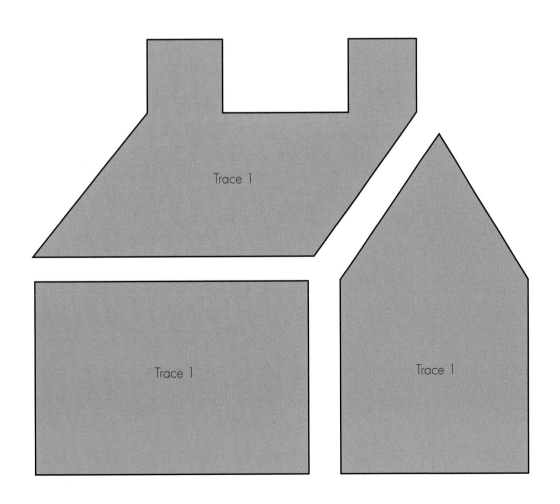

Trace 1

Trace 1

Trace 1

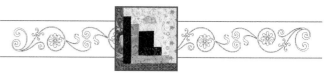

Bittersweet
Table Topper

Finished Table Topper Size: 24-1/2" x 36-1/2"

No matter your preference in home design, a log cabin piece warms both a traditonal and contemporary table top.

Materials

- (1) dark value fat eighth
- (10) assorted light value 1-1/2" x 21" strips
- (6) assorted dark value fat quarters **OR** (64) 1-1/2" x 21" strips
- 5" square orange wool
- 4" square rust wool
- 3-1/2" square gold wool
- 1/3 yard black fabric
- 7/8 yard backing fabric
- 32" x 42" piece batting
- Green and brown #8 perle cotton
- Freezer paper

Read through Making Blocks with the 6" Log Cabin Trim Tool and Chain Piecing Log Cabin Blocks on pages 6-27 before beginning.

wof = width of fabric

Fat eighth = 9" x 22"

Fat quarter = 18" x 22"

Cutting

From dark value fat eighth, cut:
    (3) 2" x wof strips. From the strips, cut:
        (24) 2" center squares

From **each** light value fat quarter, cut:
    (2) 1-1/2" x wof strips

From **each** dark value fat quarter, cut:
    (12) 1-1/2" x wof strips

From black fabric, cut:
    (4) 2-1/4" x wof binding strips

Making the Blocks

Note: Refer to pages 6-8 and 18-21 to sew the Log Cabin Blocks.

1. Sew a 2" dark center square to a 1-1/2" light strip, right sides together. Trim the light strip even with the center square and press the seam.

2. Sew the segment from step 1 to another 1-1/2" light strip, right sides together. The light strips should be sewn in a clockwise rotation on adjacent sides of the dark center square. Trim the light strip even with the center square and press the seam.

3. In the same manner, sew two dark strips to the remaining sides of the center square to complete Round 1. Press the block and trim Round 1 to size using the 6" Log Cabin Trim Tool.

4. Referring to steps 2-3, sew Rounds 2 and 3 to the block. Press and trim the block after each round is added. Make 8 light/dark Log Cabin Blocks.

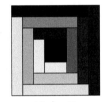

Make 8

5. Referring to steps 1-4 and using only dark strips, make a total of 16 dark Log Cabin Blocks.

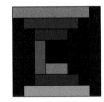

Make 16

Note: The border of this table topper is created by sewing Log Cabin Blocks with all medium and dark logs. This treatment can be used for any quilt and is a great way to use up your scraps.

Table Topper Assembly

1. Lay out 6 dark Log Cabin Blocks in a row. Sew the blocks together to make an outer row. Make 2 outer rows. Press the seams in one row to the left and the seams in the other row to the right.

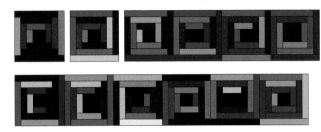

Make 2

2. Lay out 4 light/dark and 2 dark Log Cabin Blocks in a row as shown. Sew the blocks together to make a center row. Make 2 center rows. Press the seams in one row to the left and the seams in the other row to the right.

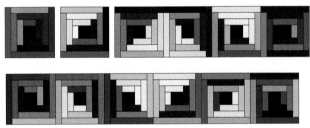

Make 2

3. Lay out the outer rows and center rows as shown. Sew the rows together, nesting the seams, to complete the table topper top. Press the seams in one direction.

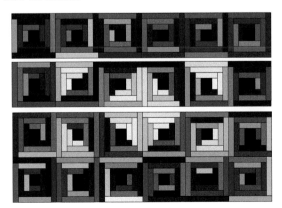

Adding the Appliqué

1. Trace the appliqué shapes onto the matte side of the freezer paper. Cut out the shapes.

2. Press the shiny side of the freezer paper to the appropriate color wool squares. Cut out the wool shapes.

Note: The freezer paper will help stabilize the wool making it easier to cut.

3. Referring to the diagram as a guide, position the wool shapes on the pieced rows. Remove the freezer paper and glue the wool pieces in place using water-soluble glue.

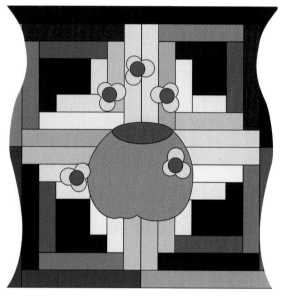

4. Appliqué the shapes in place using a blind stitch.

Finishing

1. Using a water-soluble marker, draw the flower stems, curlicues and pumpkin segments. Buttonhole stitch around the pumpkin. Use a running stitch to create the pumpkin segments and stem stitch the vines.

2. Layer the table topper top, batting and backing. Quilt as desired.

3. Sew the binding strips together along the short ends to make one strip. Press seams open.

4. Press the strip in half lengthwise, wrong sides together, and sew to the raw edge of the table topper top. Fold binding strip over raw edge and hand stitch in place.

Templates are full-size

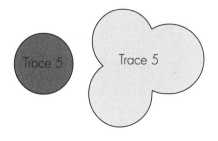

Trace 5

Trace 5

Trace 1

Templates are full-size

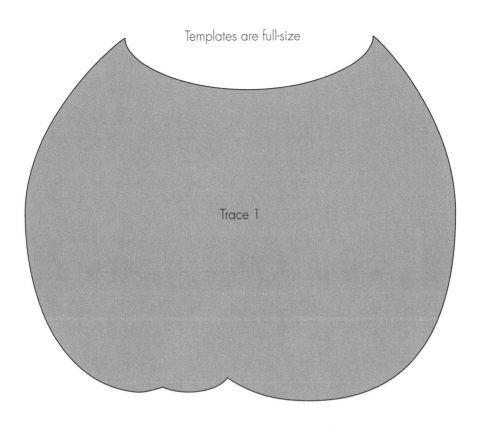

Trace 1

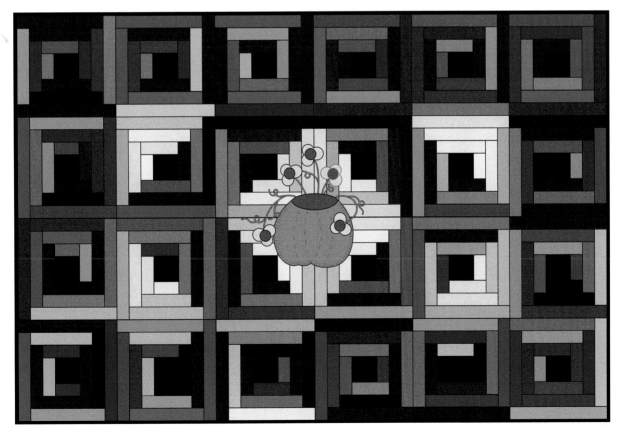

Bittersweet Table Topper
Finished Table Topper Size: 24-1/2" x 36-1/2"

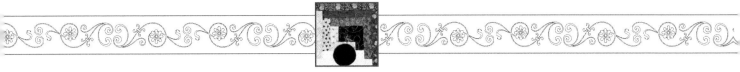

Pathway Home Quilt

Finished Quilt Size: 69-1/2" x 89-1/2"

Legend has it that during the Civil War, log cabin quilts were used as signposts for safe houses. A log cabin quilt hung in a window might mean the house was a safe place to stop. Without it one would continue on their journey. The circles on this quilt give a more contemporary look to the very traditional quilt.

Materials

- (22) assorted dark value fat quarters **OR** approximately 5-1/2 yards of scraps

- (16) assorted light value fat quarters **OR** approximately 4 yards of scraps

- 1 yard dark red fabric

- 1 yard medium brown fabric

- Assorted wool scraps in a variety of colors

- 5-1/3 yards 42"-wide fabric for backing **OR** 2-1/8 yards 108"-wide fabric

- Full-size batting

- Freezer paper

Read through Making Block with the 6" Log Cabin Trim Tool and Chain Piecing Log Cabin Blocks on pages 6-27 before beginning.

wof = width of fabric

Fat quarter = 18" x 22"

Cutting

From the freezer paper, cut:
> (38) chevron shapes and a variety of circles using the templates on page 48. You will need (41) 1-1/2" circles for the outer border and approximately 200 circles in varying sizes for the quilt top.

From 2 dark value fat quarters, cut:
> (14) 2" x wof strips. From the strips, cut:
> > (140) 2" center squares

From the remaining dark value fat quarters, cut:
> (38) chevron shapes from the longest edge of the fat quarters. Iron the shiny side of the chevron freezer paper shapes to the fat quarters before cutting.
>
> Cut the remaining pieces into 1-1/2" x wof strips

From **each** light value fat quarter, cut:
> (12) 1-1/2" x wof strips

From dark red fabric, cut:
> (8) 1-1/4" x wof inner border strips
> (9) 2-1/4" x wof binding strips

From medium brown fabric, cut:
> (7) 4-1/2" x wof outer border strips

Making the Blocks

Note: Refer to pages 6-8 and 18-21 to sew the Log Cabin Blocks.

1. Sew a 2" dark center square to a 1-1/2" light strip, right sides together. Trim the light strip even with the center square and press the seam.

2. Sew the segment from step 1 to another 1-1/2" light strip, right sides together. The strips should be sewn in a clockwise rotation on adjacent sides of the dark center square. Trim the light strip even with the center square and press the seam.

3. In the same manner, sew two dark strips to the remaining two sides of the center square to complete Round 1. Press the block and trim Round 1 to size using the 6" Log Cabin Trim Tool.

4. Referring to steps 2-3, sew Rounds 2 and 3 to the block. Press and trim the block after each round is added. Make 140 light/dark Log Cabin Blocks.

Make 140

Row Assembly

1. Lay out the blocks in 14 rows with 10 blocks in each row. Carefully watch the orientation of the blocks.

2. Sew the blocks together in rows. Press the seams in the odd numbered rows to the left and the seams in the even numbered rows to the right.

3. Sew the rows together in pairs, nesting the seams. Make 7 row pairs.

Adding the Quilt Center Appliqués

1. Press the shiny side of the freezer paper circles to the scraps of wool. Cut out the wool circles. Remove the freezer paper. Set aside (41) 1-1/2" wool circles for the outer border.

Note: The freezer paper will help stabilize the wool making it easier to cut.

2. Using water-soluble glue, glue 1-2 wool circles on each block in the row pairs, at least 1/4" away from the edge of the block. Appliqué the circles in place using a blind stitch.

Quilt Center Assembly

1. Referring to the Quilt Center Assembly Diagram, lay out the row pairs as shown.

2. Sew the pairs together to complete the quilt center. Add additional wool circles over the seams if desired.

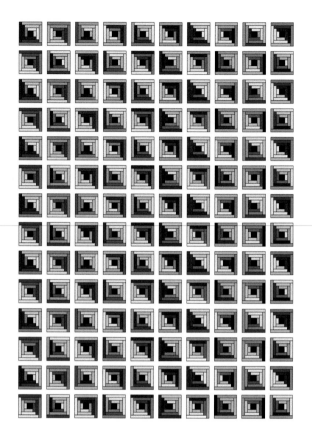

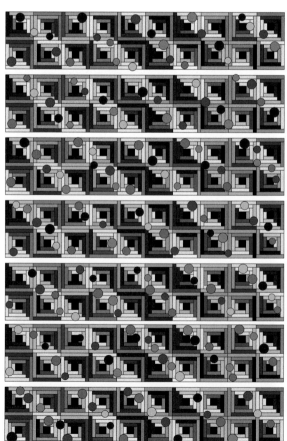

Quilt Center Assembly Diagram

Adding the Borders

Inner Border

1. Sew the 1-1/4" dark red inner border strips together on the diagonal to make one strip. Press seams open.

2. Layer one long edge of the quilt center on the inner border strip, right sides together. Sew the pieces together and trim the inner border strip even with the quilt center. Repeat on the opposite side of the quilt center. Press seams toward inner border.

Note: Sewing with the quilt center on top of the inner border strips helps control the seams in the block rows.

3. In the same manner, sew the inner border to the top and bottom of the quilt center.

Outer Border

Note: The outer border is sewn to three sides.

1. Sew the 4-1/2" medium brown outer border strips together on the diagonal to make one strip. Press seams open.

2. Measure the length of the quilt center and cut two side border strips to that length. The side border strips should measure approximately 86". Sew the side border strips to opposite sides of the quilt center, right sides together. Press seams toward inner border.

3. In the same manner, Measure the width of the quilt center including the side borders and cut a bottom border strip to that length. The bottom border strip should measure approximately 70". Sew the strip to bottom of the quilt center, right sides together. Press seams toward inner border.

Adding the Outer Border Appliqués

1. Using a water-soluble marker, draw a vertical line on the outer border every 6". Follow the seam lines of the quilt center.

2. Center the chevron appliqués between the drawn lines. Place the "V" of the chevrons 1/2" from the bottom edge of the outer border.

3. Position and glue the 1-1/2" wool circles over the raw edges of the chevrons. Blind stitch all the appliqués in place.

Finishing

1. Layer the quilt top, batting and backing. Quilt as desired.

2. Sew the binding strips together along the short ends to make one strip. Press seams open.

3. Press the strip in half lengthwise, wrong sides together. Sew to the raw edge of the quilt top. Fold binding strip over raw edge and hand stitch in place.

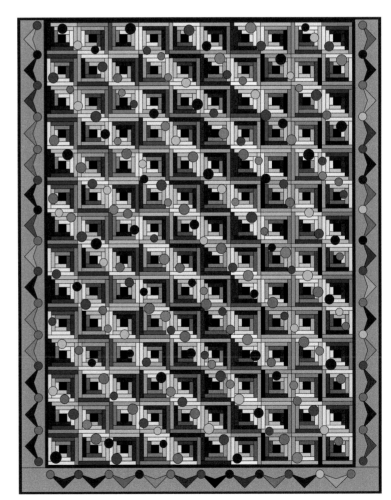

Pathway Home Quilt
Finished Quilt Size: 69-1/2" x 89-1/2"

Templates are full-size

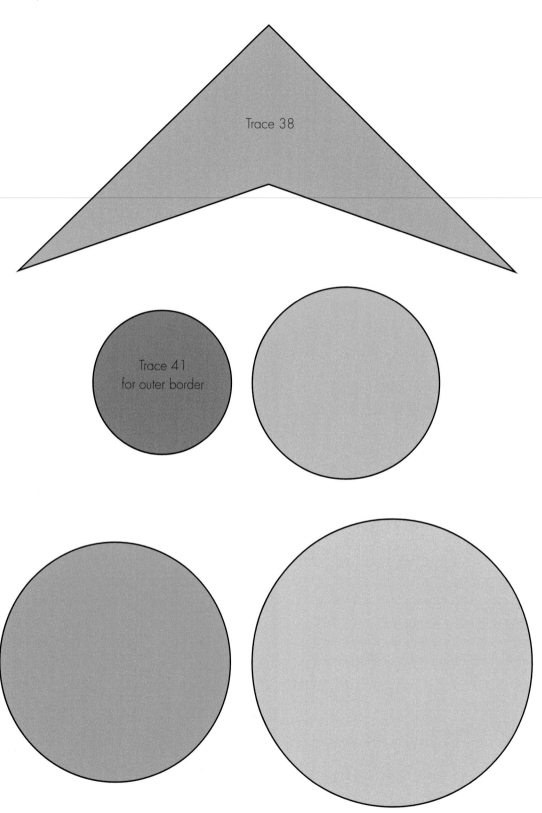

Trace 38

Trace 41
for outer border

Trace a total of 200 circles in various sizes
This is in addition to the 41 circles for the outer border

Optional Sizes for Pathway Home Quilt

Table Topper	Throw	Queen
Finished size: 45-1/2" Square Note: The table topper has an outer border on all four sides. **Make 36 blocks** **Table Topper has 6 rows with 6 blocks in each row** (1) dark fat eighth, cut: 　(36) 2" center squares (8) assorted light value fat quarters, cut: 　(12) 1-1/2" x wof strips (10) assorted dark value fat quarters, cut: 　(24) chevrons 　remaining fabric into 　1-1/2" x wof strips 1/2 yard inner border and binding fabric, cut: 　(4) 1-1/4" x wof strips 　(5) 2-1/4" x wof strips 2/3 yard outer border fabric, cut: 　(5) 4-1/2" x wof strips 1/4 yard assorted wool scraps, cut: 　(48) assorted size circles 　for quilt center 　(28) border circles 3 yards backing fabric	Finished size: 57-1/2" x 65-1/2" **Make 80 blocks** **Throw has 10 rows with 8 blocks in each row** (1) dark fat quarter, cut: 　(80) 2" center squares (12) assorted light value fat quarters, cut: 　(12) 1-1/2" x wof strips (14) assorted dark value fat quarters, cut: 　(28) chevrons 　remaining fabric into 　1-1/2" x wof strips 3/4 yard inner border and binding fabric, cut: 　(5) 1-1/4" x wof strips 　(7) 2-1/4" x wof strips 2/3 yard outer border fabric, cut: 　(5) 4-1/2" x wof strips 1/3 yard assorted wool scraps, cut: 　(120) assorted size circles 　for quilt center 　(31) border circles 3-1/2 yards backing fabric	Finished size: 95-1/2" x 100-3/4" **Make 224 blocks** **Quilt has 16 rows with 14 blocks in each row** (3) dark fat quarters, cut: 　(224) 2" center squares (30) assorted light value fat quarters, cut: 　(12) 1-1/2" x wof strips (34) assorted dark value fat quarters, cut: 　(46) chevrons 　remaining fabric into 　1-1/2" x wof strips 1-1/8 yard inner border and binding fabric, cut: 　(8) 1-1/4" x wof strips 　(11) 2-1/4" x wof strips 1-1/8 yards outer border fabric, cut: 　(8) 4-1/2" x wof strips 1 yard assorted wool scraps, cut: 　(300) assorted size 　circles for quilt center 　(49) border circles 9 yards 42"-wide **OR** 3 yards 　108"-wide backing fabric

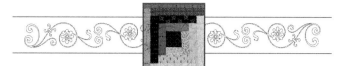

Scrappy Log Cabin Pillow

Pillow Size: 24" square

Materials

- (1) dark value 2" x wof strip
- (12) assorted light value 1-1/2" x wof strips
- (16) assorted dark value 1-1/2" x wof strips
- 1/2 yard 54"-wide Cuddle Suede **OR**
  1 yard 45"-wide pillow backing fabric
- 30" square pillow top backing fabric
- 30" square batting
- 24" pillow form

Refer to Making Blocks with the 6" Log Cabin Trim Tool and Chain Piecing Log Cabin Blocks on pages 6-27 before beginning.

wof = width of fabric

Cutting

From dark value 2" x wof strip, cut:
(16) 2" center squares

From pillow backing fabric, cut:
(2) 16" x 24-1/2" backing pieces

Making the Blocks

Note: Refer to pages 6-8 and 18-21 to sew the Log Cabin Blocks.

1. Sew a 2" dark center square to a 1-1/2" light strip, right sides together. Trim the light strip even with the center square and press the seam.

2. Sew the segment from step 1 to another 1-1/2" light strip, right sides together. The light strips should be sewn in a clockwise rotation on adjacent sides of the dark center square. Trim the light strip even with the center square and press the seam.

3. In the same manner, sew two dark strips to the remaining sides of the center square to complete Round 1. Press the block and trim Round 1 to size using the 6" Log Cabin Trim Tool.

4. Referring to steps 2-3, sew Rounds 2 and 3 to the block. Press and trim the block after each round is added. Make 16 light/dark Log Cabin Blocks.

Pillow Top Assembly

1. Lay out the Log Cabin Blocks in 4 rows with 4 blocks in each row. Carefully watch the orientation of the blocks.

2. Sew the blocks together in rows. Press the seams in the odd numbered rows to the left and the seams in the even numbered rows to the right.

3. Sew the rows together, nesting the seams. Press the seams in one direction to complete the pillow top.

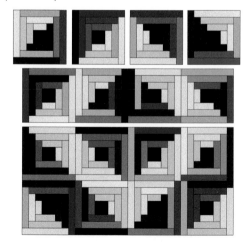

4. Layer the pillow top, batting and pillow top backing together. Quilt as desired.

5. Trim the pillow top backing and batting even with the pillow top. It should measure approximately 24-1/2" square.

Finishing

1. Turn under one edge of a pillow backing piece approximately 1/4" along the 24-1/2" side. Turn the same edge under again approximately 2" and press. Edge stitch along the outer edges of the flap to hold it in place. Repeat with the remaining pillow backing piece.

2. Place the quilted pillow top right side up on a flat surface. Lay the pillow backing pieces on the quilted pillow top, right sides together. Overlap the pillow backing pieces, adjusting as needed. Trim any excess fabric that is not covering the pillow top.

3. Pin and stitch the pieces together around the outside edge. Trim the corners.

4. Turn the pillow right side out. Press and insert the pillow form.

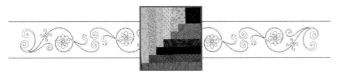

Scrappy Half Log Cabin Pillow

Pillow Size: 24" square

Materials

- (1) dark value 2" x wof strip
- (12) assorted light value 1-1/2" x wof strips
- (16) assorted dark value 1-1/2" x wof strips
- 1/2 yard 54"-wide Cuddle Suede **OR**
  1 yard 45"-wide pillow backing fabric
- 30" square pillow top backing fabric
- 30" square batting
- 24" pillow form

Refer to Making Blocks with the 6" Log Cabin Trim Tool and Chain Piecing Log Cabin Blocks on pages 6-27 before beginning.

wof = width of fabric

Cutting

From dark value 2" x wof strip, cut:
   (16) 2" corner squares

From pillow backing fabric, cut:
   (2) 16" x 24-1/2" backing pieces

Making the Blocks

Note: Refer to pages 12-17 and 24-27 to sew the Half Log Cabin Blocks.

1. Sew a 2" dark center square to a 1-1/2" light strip, right sides together. Trim the light strip even with the corner square and press the seam.

2. Sew the segment from step 1 to a 1-1/2" dark strip, right sides together. The strips should be sewn in a clockwise rotation on adjacent sides of the dark corner square. Trim the dark strip even with the corner square to complete Round 1.

3. Press the block and trim Round 1 to size using the 6" Log Cabin Trim Tool.

4. Referring to steps 2-3, sew Rounds 2-6 to the block. Press and trim the block after each round is added. Make 16 Half Log Cabin Blocks.

Pillow Top Assembly

1. Lay out the Half Log Cabin Blocks in 4 rows with 4 blocks in each row. Carefully watch the orientation of the blocks.

2. Sew the blocks together in rows. Press the seams in the odd numbered rows to the left and the seams in the even numbered rows to the right.

3. Sew the rows together, nesting the seams. Press the seams in one direction to complete the pillow top.

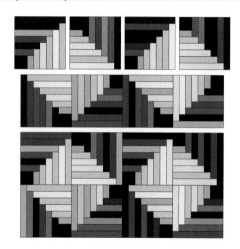

4. Layer the pillow top, batting and pillow top backing together. Quilt as desired.

5. Trim the pillow top backing and batting even with the pillow top. It should measure approximately 24-1/2" square.

Finishing

1. Turn under one edge of a pillow backing piece approximately 1/4" along the 24-1/2" side. Turn the same edge under again approximately 2" and press. Edge stitch along the outer edges of the flap to hold it in place. Repeat with the remaining pillow backing piece.

2. Place the quilted pillow top right side up on a flat surface. Lay the pillow backing pieces on the quilted pillow top, right sides together. Overlap the pillow backing pieces, adjusting as needed. Trim any excess fabric that is not covering the pillow top.

3. Pin and stitch the pieces together around the outside edge. Trim the corners.

4. Turn the pillow right side out. Press and insert the pillow form.

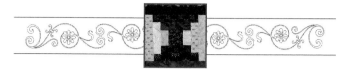

Scrappy Courthouse Steps Pillow
Pillow Size: 24" square

Materials

- (1) dark value 2" x wof strip
- (12) assorted light value 1-1/2" x wof strips
- (16) assorted dark value 1-1/2" x wof strips
- 1/2 yard 54"-wide Cuddle Suede **OR** 1 yard 45"-wide pillow backing fabric
- 30" square pillow top backing fabric
- 30" square batting
- 24" pillow form

Refer to *Making Blocks with the 6" Log Cabin Trim Tool* and *Chain Piecing Log Cabin Blocks* on pages 6-27 before beginning.

wof = width of fabric

Cutting

From dark value 2" x wof strip, cut:
    (16) 2" center squares

From pillow backing fabric, cut:
    (2) 16" x 24-1/2" backing pieces

Making the Blocks

Note: Refer to pages 9-11 and 22-27 to sew the Courthouse Steps Blocks.

1. Sew a 1-1/2" light strip to a 2" dark center square, right sides together. Trim the light strip even with the center square and press the seam. Sew another 1-1/2" light strip to the opposite side of the center square in the same manner.

2. Sew dark strips to opposite sides of the segment in step 1 to complete Round 1. Press the block and trim Round 1 using the 6" Log Cabin Trim Tool.

3. Referring to steps 1-2, sew Rounds 2 and 3 to the block. Press and trim the block after each round is added. Make 16 Courthouse Steps Blocks.

Pillow Top Assembly

1. Lay out the Courthouse Steps Blocks in 4 rows with 4 blocks in each row. The blocks should be oriented the same in each row.

2. Sew the blocks together in rows. Press the seams in the odd numbered rows to the left and the seams in the even numbered rows to the right.

3. Sew the rows together, nesting the seams. Press the seams in one direction to complete the pillow top.

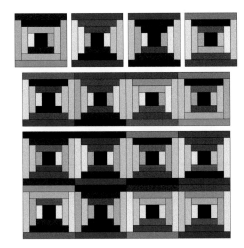

4. Layer the pillow top, batting and pillow top backing together. Quilt as desired.

5. Trim the pillow top backing and batting even with the pillow top. It should measure approximately 24-1/2" square.

Finishing

1. Turn under one edge of a pillow backing piece approximately 1/4" along the 24-1/2" side. Turn the same edge under again approximately 2" and press. Edge stitch along the outer edges of the flap to hold it in place. Repeat with the remaining pillow backing piece.

2. Place the quilted pillow top right side up on a flat surface. Lay the pillow backing pieces on the quilted pillow top, right sides together. Overlap the pillow backing pieces, adjusting as needed. Trim any excess fabric that is not covering the pillow top.

3. Pin and stitch the pieces together around the outside edge. Trim the corners.

4. Turn the pillow right side out. Press and insert the pillow form.

In the Pocket Table Square

Table Square Size: 24-1/2" square

A recyled jeans pocket adds a little quirkiness to this table square. It's not something our great-grandmothers would have done, but it's nice to change up tradition.

Materials

- (1) medium blue fat eighth
- (6) assorted light value fat quarters **OR** (20) 1-1/2" x 21" strips
- (6) assorted dark value fat quarters **OR** at least (24) 1-1/2" x 21" strips
- Assorted gold wool scrapsl
- 1/4 yard dark blue fabric
- 7/8 yard backing fabric
- 28-1/2" square of batting
- Green #8 perle cotton
- 3/4 yard 3/8" green ribbon
- 3 medium blue buttons
- 4" square jean pocket or any pocket size that will fit within the light center square
- Freezer paper

Read through Making Blocks with the 6" Log Cabin Trim Tool and Chain Piecing Log Cabin Blocks on pages 6-27 before beginning.

wof = width of fabric

Fat eighth = 9" x 22"

Fat Quarter = 18" x 22"

Cutting

From medium blue fat eighth, cut:
    (2) 2" x wof strips. From the strips, cut:
        (16) 2" center squares

From assorted light value fat quarters, cut:
    (20) 1-1/2" x wof strips

From assorted dark value fat quarters, cut:
    (24) 1-1/2" x wof strips

From dark blue fabric, cut:
    (3) 2-1/4" x wof binding strips

Making the Blocks

Note: Refer to pages 6-8 and 18-21 to sew the Log Cabin Blocks.

1. Sew a 2" medium blue center square to a 1-1/2" light strip, right sides together. Trim the light strip even with the center square and press the seam.

2. Sew the segment from step 1 to another 1-1/2" light strip, right sides together. The strips should be sewn in a clockwise rotation on adjacent sides of the medium blue center square. Trim the light strip even with the center square and press the seam.

3. In the same manner, sew two dark strips to the remaining two sides of the center square to complete Round 1. Press the block and trim Round 1 to size using the 6" Log Cabin Trim Tool.

4. Referring to steps 2-3, sew Rounds 2 and 3 to the block. Press and trim the block after each round is added. Make 16 light/dark Log Cabin Blocks.

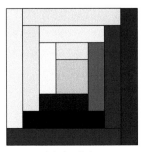

Make 16

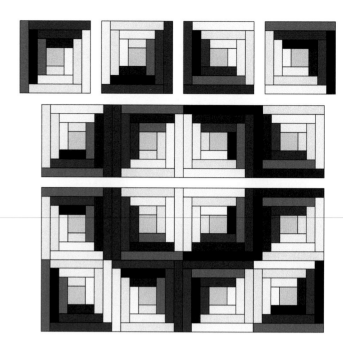

Table Square Assembly

1. Lay out the Log Cabin Blocks in 4 rows with 4 blocks in each row as shown. Carefully watch the orientation of the blocks.

2. Sew the blocks together in rows. Press the seams in the odd numbered rows to the left and the seams in the even numbered rows to the right.

3. Sew the rows together, nesting the seams, to complete the table square top. Press the seams in one direction.

Adding the Appliqué

1. Trace the appliqué shape on page 57 onto the matte side of the freezer paper. Cut out the shapes.

2. Press the shiny side of the freezer paper shapes to the gold wool. Cut out the wool shapes.

3. Referring to the photo on page 54 and the diagram on page 57, position the wool shapes and pocket on the table square top. Remove the freezer paper and glue the wool pieces in place using water-soluble glue.

4. Appliqué the shapes in place using a blind stitch. Sew the pocket top closed.

Finishing

1. Using a water soluble marker, draw the flower stems. Using a stem stitch, embroider the stems. Make a bow with the green ribbon and tack it in place on the pocket. Sew a button to the center of each flower.

2. Layer the table square top, batting and backing. Quilt as desired.

3. Sew the binding strips together along the short ends to make one strip. Press seams open.

4. Press the strip in half lengthwise, wrong sides together, and sew to the raw edge of the table square. Fold binding strip over raw edge and hand stitch in place.

Template is full-size

Trace 15 for table square
Trace 50 for place mats

Stem Stitch

Pocket Full of Posies Table Square
Table Square Size: 24-1/2" square

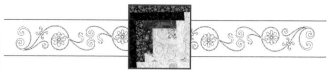

In the Pocket Place Mats

Place Mat Size: 12-1/2" x 18-1/2"

In this upcycled jeans pocket, flowers find a home as well as a knife, fork, and spoon with a log cabin table setting.

Materials

Makes 2 place mats

- (1) medium blue fat eighth
- (6) assorted light value fat quarters **OR** (20) 1-1/2" x 21" strips
- (6) assorted dark value fat quarters **OR** (20) 1-1/2" x 21" strips
- Assorted gold wool scraps
- 1/8 yard dark blue fabric
- 1/2 yard backing fabric
- (2) 14" x 20" pieces of batting
- Green and blue #8 perle cotton
- 1 yard 3/8" green ribbon
- (2) 4" square jean pockets

Freezer paper

Read through Making Blocks with the 6" Log Cabin Trim Tool and Chain Piecing Log Cabin Blocks on pages 6-27 before beginning.

wof = width of fabric

Fat eighth = 9" x 22"

Fat Quarter = 18" x 22"

Cutting

From medium blue fat eighth, cut:
  (2) 2" x wof strips. From the strips, cut:
    (12) 2" center squares

From assorted light value fat quarters, cut:
  (20) 1-1/2" x wof strips

From assorted dark value fat quarters, cut:
  (20) 1-1/2" x wof strips

From dark blue fabric, cut:
  (4) 2-1/4" x wof binding strips

Making the Blocks

Note: Refer to pages 6-8 and 18-21 to sew the Log Cabin Blocks.

1. Sew a 2" medium blue center square to a 1-1/2" light strip, right sides together. Trim the light strip even with the center square and press the seam.

2. Sew the segment from step 1 to another 1-1/2" light strip, right sides together. The strips should be sewn in a clockwise rotation on adjacent sides of the medium blue center square. Trim the light strip even with the center square and press the seam.

3. In the same manner, sew two dark strips to the remaining two sides of the center square to complete Round 1. Press the block and trim Round 1 to size using the 6" Log Cabin Trim Tool.

4. Referring to steps 2-3, sew Rounds 2 and 3 to the block. Press and trim the block after each round is added. Make 8 light/dark Log Cabin Blocks.

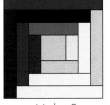

Make 8

5. Referring to steps 1-4 and using only light strips, make 4 light Log Cabin Blocks.

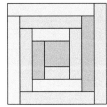

Make 4

Place Mat Assembly

1. Lay out 4 light/dark and 2 light Log Cabin Blocks in 2 rows as shown.

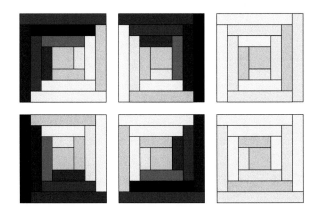

2. Sew the blocks together in rows. Press the seams in one row to the left and the seams in the other row to the right.

3. Sew the rows together, nesting the seams, to complete a place mat top. Press the seams in one direction. Make 2 place mat tops.

Adding the Appliqué

1. Trace the appliqué shape on page 57 onto the matte side of the freezer paper. Cut out the shapes.

2. Press the shiny side of the freezer paper shapes to the gold wool. Cut out the wool shapes.

3. Referring to the photo on page 58, position the wool shapes and pocket on the place mat tops. Remove the freezer paper and glue the pieces in place using water-soluble glue.

4. Appliqué the shapes in place using a blind stitch. Leave the pocket open for a napkin.

Finishing

1. Using a water soluble marker, draw the flower stems. Using a stem stitch, embroider the stems. Embroider three French Knots to the center of each flower. Make a bow with the green ribbon and tack it in place on the pocket.

French Knot

2. Layer the place mat top, batting and backing. Quilt as desired.

3. Sew 2 binding strips together along the short ends to make one strip. Press seams open.

4. Press the strip in half lengthwise, wrong sides together, and sew to the raw edge of a place mat. Fold binding strip over raw edge and hand stitch in place.

5. Repeat steps 1-4 to finish the remaining place mat.

Grecian Squares Quilt

Finished Quilt Size: 73-1/2" x 97-1/2"

The log cabin block was historically made from scraps. The shape of the log is very geometric, much like today's abstract and contemporary art. When planned colors and design are applied to the block, the "old" becomes the "new" and a quilt of Log Cabin Blocks can suddenly become fine art.

Materials

- 6-3/4 yards light fabric
- 2/3 yard dark fabric
- (48-54) assorted dark value fat eighths **OR** (24-26) fat quarters
- 1/3 yard dark red fabric
- Assorted wool scraps in a variety of colors
- 2/3 yard binding fabric
- 6 yards 42"-wide **OR** 3 yards 90"-wide **OR** 2-1/4 yards 108"-wide fabric for backing
- Queen-size batting

Read through Making Blocks with the 6" Log Cabin Trim Tool and Chain Piecing Log Cabin Blocks on pages 6-27 before beginning.

wof = width of fabric

Fat eighth = 9" x 22"

Cutting

From light fabric, cut:
(7) 2" x wof strips for the center squares

(106) 1-1/2" x wof strips. From 1 strip, cut:
(2) 1-1/2" x 10" strips for border corners

(10) 2" x wof strips. From 1 strip, cut:
(4) 2" x 6-1/2" rectangles for border corners
(4) 2" x 3-1/2" rectangles for border corners

(12) 2-3/4" x wof strips for outer border

From dark fabric, cut:
(10) 2" x wof strips for the center squares and border.
From 1 strip, cut:
(1) 2" x 10" strip for border corners

From assorted dark value fat eighths, cut:
1-1/2" x 22" strips

From dark red fabric, cut:
(8) 1-1/4" x wof inner border strips

From assorted wool scraps, cut:
(122) 1" squares

From binding fabric, cut:
(9) 2-1/4" x wof strips

Making the Blocks

Note: Refer to pages 9-11 and 22-27 to sew the Courthouse Steps Blocks.

Dark Center Courthouse Steps Blocks

1. Sew a 1-1/2" light strip to both sides of a 2" dark strip, right sides together. Press the seams toward the light strips. Cut this strip set into 2"-wide segments. Make three more strips sets and cut into 2"-wide segments for a total of 70 segments.

Make 70

2. Sew 1-1/2" light strips to opposite sides of a segment from step 1 to complete Round 1. Press the block and trim Round 1 to size using the 6" Log Cabin Trim Tool.

3. Referring to steps 1-2, sew Rounds 2 and 3 to the block using dark strips for Round 2 and light strips for Round 3. Press and trim the block after each round is added. Make 70 dark center Courthouse Steps Blocks.

Make 70

Make 70

Light Center Courthouse Steps Blocks

1. Sew a 1-1/2" dark strip to both sides of a 2" light strip, right sides together. Press the seams toward the dark strips. Cut this strip set into 2"-wide segments. Make five more strips sets and cut into 2"-wide segments for a total of 122 segments.

Make 122

2. Sew 1-1/2" dark strips to opposite sides of a segment from step 1 to complete Round 1. Press the block and trim Round 1 to size using the 6" Log Cabin Trim Tool. Make 122 Round 1 Units. Set 52 Round 1 Units aside to be used in outer border.

Make 122

3. Referring to steps 1-2, sew Rounds 2 and 3 to the remaining 70 Round 1 Units using light strips for Round 2 and dark strips for Round 3. Press and trim the blocks after each round is added. Make 70 light center Courthouse Steps Blocks.

Make 70

Row Assembly

1. Lay out the blocks in 14 rows with 10 blocks in each row. The dark and light center blocks will alternate within each row.

2. Sew the blocks together in rows. Press the seams in the odd numbered rows to the left and the seams in the even numbered rows to the right.

3. Sew the rows together in pairs, nesting the seams. The odd rows should begin with a light center block and the even rows should begin with a dark center block. Make 7 row pairs.

Adding the Quilt Center Appliqué

1. Center a 1" wool square on the center of each light center Courthouse Steps Blocks. Glue the squares in place.

2. Appliqué the squares in place using a blind stitch.

Quilt Center Assembly

1. Referring to the diagram on page 62, lay out the row pairs as shown.

2. Sew the pairs together to complete the quilt center.

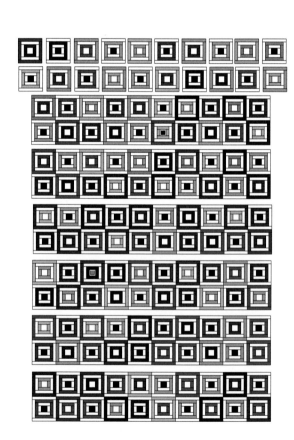

Adding the Borders

Inner Border

1. Sew the 1-1/4" dark red inner border strips together on the diagonal to make one strip. Press the seams open.

2. Layer one long edge of the quilt center on the inner border strip, right sides together. Sew the pieces together and trim the inner border strip even with the quilt center. Repeat on the opposite side of the quilt center. Press seams toward inner border.

Note: Sewing with the quilt center on top of the inner border strips helps control the seams in the block rows.

3. In the same manner, sew the inner border to the top and bottom of the quilt center.

Outer Border

1. Appliqué 1" wool squares to the centers of the remaining 52 Round 1 Units. Set aside 4 Round 1 Units.

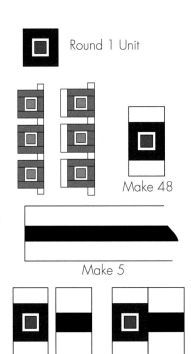

Round 1 Unit

Make 48

2. Chain piece 48 Round 1 Units on top of a 2" light strip. Trim even with sides of the pieced center. Chain piece a 2" light strip to the opposite end of the pieced unit and trim even with the pieced center. Your Round 1 Unit should now measure 3-1/2" x 6-1/2".

3. Sew 2-3/4" x wof light strips to opposite long edges of a 2" x wof dark strip. Press seams toward light strips to make a strip set. Make 5 strip sets.

Make 5

4. From the strips sets cut: (44) 3-1/2" segments, (4) 2-3/4" segments, (4) 4-1/4" segments and (4) 2" segments.

5. Sew a 3-1/2" segment to one edge of a Round 1 Unit from Step 2 to make a border block. Make 44 border blocks.

Make 44

6. Referring to Top/Bottom Border Assembly Diagram, lay out (2) 2-3/4" segments from Step 4, 9 border blocks and 1 Round 1 Unit from step 2 in a row.

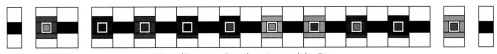

Top/Bottom Border Assembly Diagram

7. Sew the pieces together to make a top/bottom border. Make 2 top/bottom borders.

8. Sew the top/bottom borders to the top and bottom of the quilt center.

9. Referring to Side Border Assembly Diagram, lay out (2) 4-1/4" units from Step 4, 13 border blocks and 1 Round 1 Unit from step 2 in a row.

Side Border Assembly Diagram

10. Sew the pieces together to make a side border. Make 2 side borders.

Border Corners

1. Sew 1-1/2" x wof light strips to opposite long edges of a 2" x 10" dark strip. Press seams toward the dark strip to make a strip set. Cut the strip set into (4) 2" x 3-1/2" segments.

2. Lay out a Round 1 Unit, a 2" x 3-1/2" segment, a 2" x 3-1/2" light rectangle, a 2" x 6-1/2" light rectangle and a 2" segment, from step 4 above, as shown. Sew the pieces together to make a border corner. Make 4 border corners.

3. Sew a border corner to each end of the side borders, matching the dark strips.

4. Sew the side borders to opposite sides of the quilt center.

Finishing

1. Layer the quilt top, batting and backing. Quilt as desired.

2. Sew the binding strips together along the short ends to make one strip. Press seams open.

3. Press the strip in half lengthwise, wrong sides together, and sew to the raw edge of the quilt top. Fold binding strip over raw edge and hand stitch in place.

Make 4

Grecian Squares Quilt
Finished Quilt Size: 73-1/2 x 97-1/2"